Wendy Baker's...

compact Sketchbook

of blinds

157 Watchfield Court, Sutton Court Road, London W4 4NE
Telephone orders: +44(0) 845 602 1375
email:info@shoestringbooks.co.uk
website:www.shoestringbooks.co.uk

Other books by Wendy Baker

The Curtain Sketchbook	0-9532939-2-0
The Window and Bed Sketchbook	0-9532939-4-7
Curtain Recipes (Book)	0-9532939-5-5
Curtain Recipes (Cards)	0-9532939-6-3
Compact Sketchbook of Accessories	0-9532939-9-8 *

* Publication date June 2005

ILLUSTRATIONS CHRISSIE CARRIERE © FOR SHOESTRING BOOKS

Photography – Tony Cambio Images
Book Design by www.bookdesign.uk.com

ISBN 0-9532939-8-X

Conceived, edited and designed by Wendy Baker
Published by SHOESTRING BOOK COMPANY
Printed by Creative Print and Design

wendy Baker

introduction

Although curtains can look wonderful in certain cases I, as an interior designer, do prefer the simplicity of blinds and find myself incorporating them more often into my design schemes. There are some instances where blinds are a must, maybe the window is an unusual shape or perhaps there is an interesting architrave which would be a pity to cover or curtains would block out too much light...and so on.

Many of the sketches are without colour so you can choose a colour to suit your schemes, but here and there we have coloured in a few of them as it was difficult to resist the temptation!
(You can of course photocopy them in black and white if you prefer)

contents...

- window shapes

1

2

3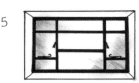

4

5

6

7

8

1. BASIC WINDOW
2. WINDOW IN RECESS
3. ROUND WINDOW
4. COTTAGE STYLE

5. 1930's FRAME
6. GEORGIAN SASH WINDOW
7. ARCHED GEORGIAN SASH
8. GOTHIC WINDOW

the basics...

-window and door shapes

1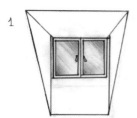

2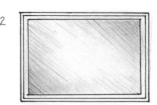

3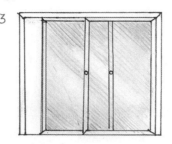

4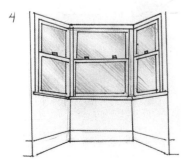

5

1. DORMER WINDOW
2. PICTURE WINDOW
3. SLIDING DOORS

4. BAY WINDOW
5. FRENCH DOORS

the basics...

- measuring up for a blind – face fix

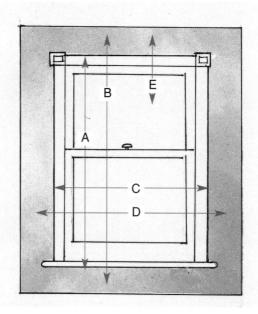

USE A METAL RETRACTABLE MEASURE FOR ACCURACY

A = THE DROP (LENGTH) FROM THE TOP OF THE ARCHITRAVE TO THE SILL.

B = THE DROP (LENGTH) FROM 20 CMS (8") ABOVE THE ARCHITRAVE TO JUST BELOW THE SILL.

C = THE WIDTH IF THE BLIND IS TO BE FIXED ON THE ARCHITRAVE.

D = THE WIDTH IF THE BLIND IS TO OVERLAP EITHER SIDE.

E = THE TOP POINT IS WHERE A POLE, PELMET OR VALANCE SHOULD BE FIXED APPROX 20 CMS (8") – THE BOTTOM POINT IS THE DROP OF THE PELMET OR VALANCE.

the basics...

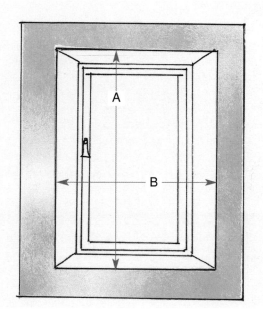

A = DROP (LENGTH)

B = THE WIDTH - TAKE THE MEASUREMENT AT THE TOP, MIDDLE AND NEAR THE BOTTOM AS WINDOWS CAN VARY IN A RECESS.

REMEMBER IF THE WINDOW OPENS INWARDS YOU CANNOT HAVE A BLIND.

making the right choice...

1. ROLLER BLINDS

   suitable for most windows – kitchens and bathrooms – bay windows with pelmets – bedroom blinds can be made light resistant – laminated translucent fabric used as a substitute for 'net' curtains – easy maintenance.

2. ROMAN BLINDS

   very popular as they can be neatly folded away – when used in bay windows it is important to pattern match – the tops can be made to fit awkward shapes with a template – suits either a traditional room setting or modern décor – borders, insets, trimmings can be added – suitable for translucent fabric.

3. AUSTRIAN BLINDS

   a 'fussy' style of blind - can look creased when in the down position – looks at its best in a traditional setting – works well in silk and brocades – best lined, and even interlined, for a more opulent look.

4. LINEN FOLD

   an alternative to 'net curtains' as the centre fabric is usually translucent – try to use a wide fabric so as not to have a join in the middle – use a heavier fabric for the two borders – this is more of a 'dress blind' than a functional one.

5. LONDON BLIND

   suitable for a traditional style room – use two contrasting fabrics especially if you are having inverted pleats – this blind looks best dressing a window as it can look very untidy when pulling it up and down.

6. FESTOONS

the only place for these blinds is in a theatre!

7. CASCADES

these are becoming quite popular as they keep their folds when in the down position – they look good when teamed up with panels and 'dress' curtains – can be made in translucent fabric but the rods do show through!

8. ORIENTAL BLIND

a simple roll-up blind which fits in very well in most room settings – use a contrast fabric instead of lining as when it is rolled up the contrast becomes a feature – match the pull cords to the contrast – easy to make and therefore inexpensive.

9. SHUTTERS

wooden indoor shutters can be made to measure and are perfect for difficult shaped windows as they can be made to fit most shapes – very popular as there are so many different combinations – natural wood or painted – they fold right back against the wall at the sides to let in the maximum of light and by adjusting the louvers you can fine tune the amount of light coming into the room.

10. VENETIANS

look best in wood - suitable for all kinds of rooms, halls, bathrooms and kitchens – perfect in metal for the workplace, as the light can be finely tuned – with bay windows but be sure to take a template of the angles of the bay for the manufacturer.

basic fabrics...

- a selection of basic fabrics

1	2	3
4	5	6
7	8	9

basic fabrics...

- selecting the right one

1. NOVELTY COTTON - Looks very effective when used as roller blind in contemporary setting.

2. OPEN WEAVES - Really more a statement than a fabric - obviously leave unlined or you loose the whole effect - excellent for panels.

3. SPOTTED VOILE - especially good used on roller blinds - a translucent fabric so Leave unlined.

4. HOROZONTAL STRIPES - use as panels or roller blinds - don't line

5. LINEN - with chenille embroidery - also comes in fantastic pane velvet

6. NATURAL SILK - keep to neutral colours.

7. COTTON - one of the least expensive fabrics on the market - excellent for any type of blind - good fabric to use for blackout blinds.

8. LINEN HERRINGBONE - most certainly one of the best fabrics to use - as well as being good to look at it is also very versatile and strong.

9. SILK - a romantic fabric and very suitable for all types of blinds - wonderful colours - line in another colour silk for an opulent effect.

natural coloured fabrics...

-teamed up with jute trimmings

houndstooth chenille...

-mixed with stripes and beads

printed linen...

-with plain linen and checked waffle cotton

a printed floral linen...

- with co-ordinating stripes, checks and beads

linen and silks...

18

co-ordinating linens...

- so crisp and simple

printed cottons...

- vibrant tones of green

printed cottons...

- a mixture of patterns

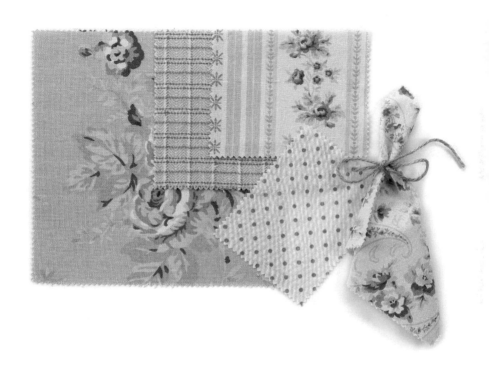

soft and delicate cottons...

-a look back into the past

faded antique linen...

-with simple pink gingham and woven silk

CABBAGES & ROSES

a mixture of different cotton prints...

delicate silks...

-together with an embroidered voile and beads

vibrant silks...

-pink and lime silks with apple blossom voile

linens with flocked velvet...

-topped with gold tassel

ribbons and braids...

You don't need to use expensive fabrics for blinds you can trim the base with a simple beaded fringe or add a flamboyant ribbon to blend in with the other soft furnishing…but don't overdo the trimmings

passementerie (trimmings)...

-a few basics

 1. GIMP

 2. PICOT RIBBON

 3. ROPE

 4. FLANGED ROPE

 5. SLOTTED HEADED FRINGE

 6. LOOP FRINGE

 7. FAN EDGE

 8. BOBBLE FRINGE

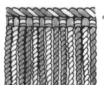 9. BULLION FRINGE

 10. CRYSTAL SATIN RIBBON

 11. BEAD FRINGE

 12. LOOPED BEADS ON GIMP

 13. STRINGS OF BEADS

 14. ASSORTED CRYSTAL BEADS ON SATIN RIBBON

 15. CUT FRINGE WITH BEADED HANGERS

jute trimmings...

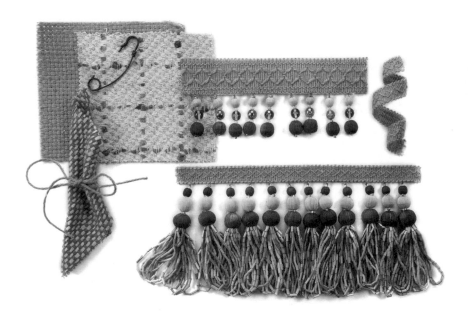

crewel work braid...

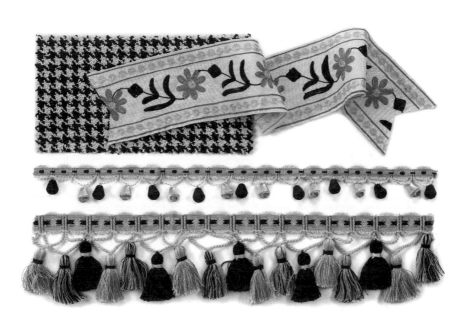

wide terracotta braid...

- with matching fringing with 'hangers'

neutral coloured trimming...

poles....(hardware)

 1. BALL

 2. PROVENCAL STYLE

 3. REEDED BALL AND POLE

 4. FLUTED BALL

 5. ACORN

 6. URN-DECORATIVE POLE

 7. TRUMPET-2 COLOURS OF WOOD

 8. ART DECO

 9. BANDED BALL- FABRIC COVERED POLE

 10. INVERTED RIB AND OGEE

 11. STYLE OF EARLY VICTORIAN SPINNING TOP

 12. LEAF AND ACORN

 13. MINARET CANDY TWIST POLE

 14. VICTORIAN SCROLL

 15. CORONET- DECORATIVE POLE

 16. OTTERMAN

poles....(hardware)

 1. STEEL SPIRE

 2. WOODEN 'BAMBOO' BALL

 3. STEEL RIBBON BALL

 4. IRON BUTTON

 5. IRON BALL

 6. IRON KNOT

 7. CAGE AND BALL

 16. SHEPHERDS CROOK

 9. ROPED BALL

 10. ROPED CONE

 11. STEEL TRUMPET

 12. STEEL CORKSCREW

 13. STEEL RIB

 14. METAL BALL

 15. STEEL SPOTTED BALL

 16. THREE TONE CONE BALLS

pull cords....

- various styles on the market

TOP RIGHT HAND SIDE IS A CLEAT - A HOOK TO
SECURE THE CORDS USED FOR WORKING THE BLIND

side winders...

- and other methods to operate a blind

1. SIDE WINDERS COME IN PLASTIC OR METAL

2. A SLOW RISER OR SPRING OPERATED PULL CORD
   (SEE OPPOSITE PAGE)

3. ELECTRIC REMOTE CONTROL MECHANISM

REMEMBER IF THE BLIND IS WIDE AND LONG IT WILL
ALSO BE HEAVY SO YOU WILL NEED HEAVY DUTY
MECHANISM...ASK YOU MANUFACTURER FOR ADVICE.

valances...

1.

2.

3.

4.

pelmets...

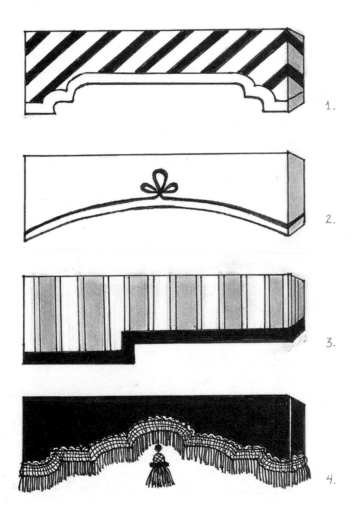

1.

2.

3.

4.

lambrequins...

1.

2.

3.

4.

fretwork...

1.

2.

a few words of advice...

An introduction to blinds

There are very few instances where blinds don't work - if the windows can't take blinds, for some reason, they more than likely won't be right for curtains either, so leave the window bare or dress the window. (See page 234)

Curtains are still most probably the best choice for a stately home or perhaps in a very traditional house as they are in keeping with the architectural style, but you can, of course, still use blinds in the kitchens and bathrooms.

If you need to create the illusion of height in a room you can use "dress curtains" together with blinds, or maybe panels which are on tracks from the ceiling.

At last there is a replacement for those ghastly "net curtains" – translucent blinds solve the problem – you can have privacy and the window is left uncluttered – a great improvement!

Wooden shutters are my favourite type of window coverings, they seem to fit into most schemes and always look good -   I love the simple lines and they can be made to fit any window in a multitude of colours... but look especially good in natural wood or simply pure white. .

Everybody has likes and dislikes but I think I have come up with enough ideas for blinds in this Sketchbook to keep everybody happy!

basic blinds...

-various styles

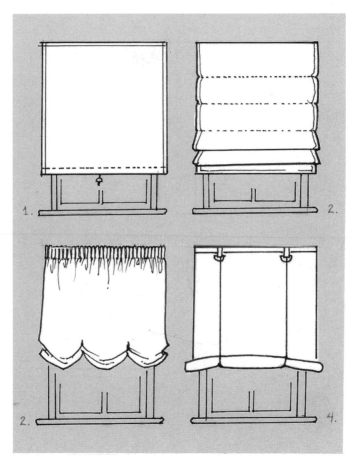

1. ROLLER
2. ROMAN
3. AUSTRIAN
4. ORIENTAL

basic blinds...

-various styles

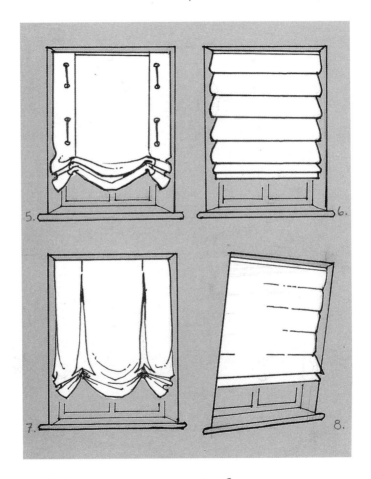

5 LONDON FOLD   6. CASCADE

7. LONDON   8. VELUX

Venetian blinds...

-wooden and metal....

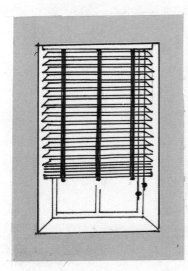

1. WOODEN

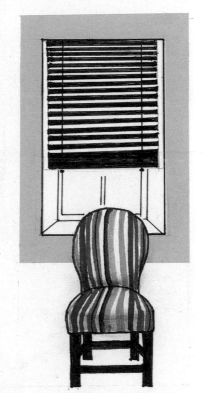

2. METAL

wooden shutters...

- for windows and doors

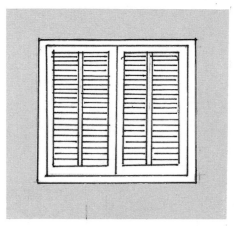

1. BASIC SHUTTERS

2. TWO TIERED

sliding panels...

- and portiéres

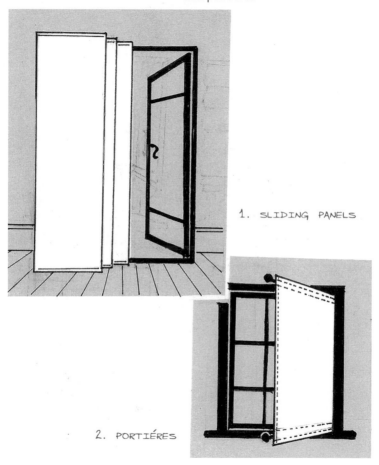

1. SLIDING PANELS

2. PORTIÉRES

dressing a window...

dressing a window...

- and after

roller blinds...

- various base shapes

Roller blinds are extremely versatile, they are suitable for most windows and can be made flame retardant and light resistant (blackout blinds) – the fabric is generally laminated which adds a coating to stiffen the fabric making it easier to roll up and down - this process works well especially on flimsy fabrics. If you are using a translucent fabric the roller blind can be left in the down position allowing light to come into the room whilst still retaining your privacy ....replacing 'net curtains.'

They can be operated by a pull cord (see page 36), a side winder (see page 37) or electrically operated.

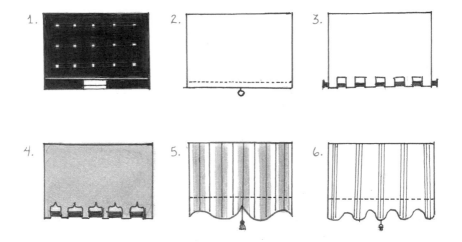

A SMALL SELECTION OF DIFFERENT SHAPED BASES AVAILABLE FROM MANUFACTURERS

- MOST FABRICS INCLUDING, OPEN WEAVE AND TRANSLUCENT ONES, ARE LAMINATED TO ADD EXTRA BODY TO THE BLIND.

roller blinds...

- a diagonal print with a tassel pull cord

roller blinds...

– with pull cord

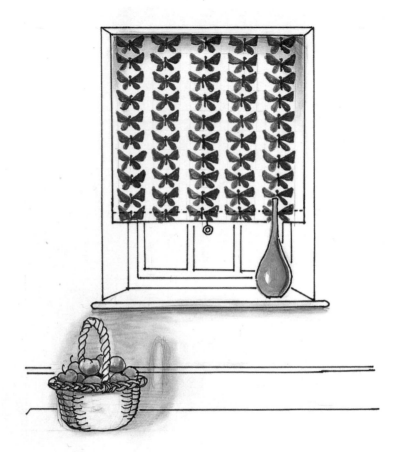

roller blinds...

- with fretwork pelmet and side winder

roller blinds...

- contemporary style

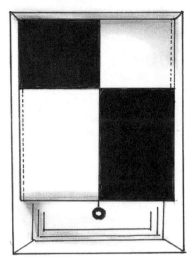

roller blinds...

— oriental influence

roller blinds...

roller blinds...

– in translucent fabric

roller blinds...

– with double lambrequin

roller blinds...

- lambrequin edged with Russian braid

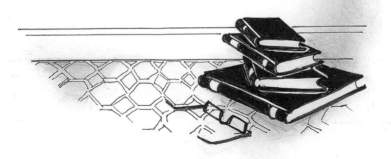

roller blinds...

Most bay windows vary slightly one way or another,
you have to decide what format works best for the
window. You can have curtains but very often this is
not possible and roller blinds seem to be the
answer, soften the window with 'dress'curtains
stacked at either side or just simply have roller blinds
on their own – perhaps have pelmets so that the
window treatment looks more complete.

Measuring correctly is very important. Give your
blind manufacturer the measurements on a flat plan
and it helps if you make a template of the angles
(this is best done from the ceiling) to eliminate any
fitting problems when installing the blinds

roller blinds...

- in this bay there is no room for curtains

roller blinds...

roller blinds...

- in a bay window

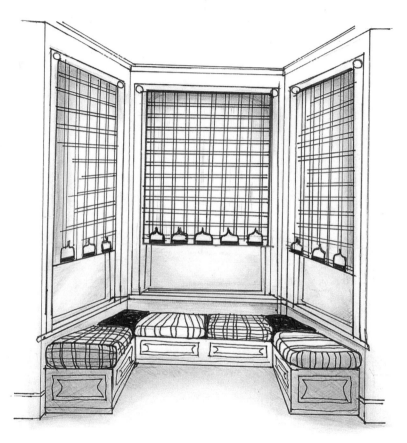

roller blinds...

- a silk dress curtain with a cut out base blind

translucent curtains...

- voile curtains and a 'blackout' blind

translucent fabric...

- with lace edging

roller blinds...

- with fretwork pelmet

roller blinds...

- simple style for a kitchen

roller blinds...

- mix and match your fabrics

roman blinds

– this blind is a softer version of a roller blind, flat when in the down position and folds up into horizontal pleats when it is up. The blind is fixed to a covered batten with the aid of a 'touch and close' tape and operated by lift cords which pass through china barrels secured by brass, chrome or wooden cleats. You can have a right or left operation.

Roman blinds tend to be the most popular type of blind, mainly because they are uncluttered and fit into most room schemes. They are generally lined, but if unlined the blind system does show through and you must have 'French seams'. Use them unlined in place of 'net' curtains for privacy.

Add borders, different headings and trimmings to compliment the other soft furnishings in the room. Remember if you have two windows side by side and you are using a print, make sure to match the print on each window.

roman blinds...

roman blinds...

- fix above the window to avoid loosing light

roman blinds...

- wide border with mitred corners

roman blinds...

- suitable for arched windows

roman blinds...

roman blinds...

roman blinds...

- in unusual places

roman blinds...

-translucent fabric

roman blinds...

-translucent fabric

roman blinds...

roman blinds...

- contemporary décor

roman blinds...

roman blinds...

-saddle stitched

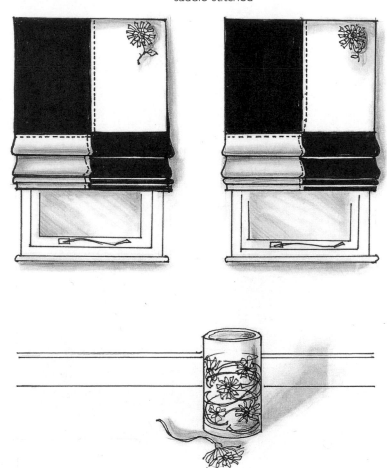

roman blinds...

- with wide border and mitred corners

roman blinds...

- a pocket headed valance

roman blinds...

roman blinds...

roman blinds...

-with a 'dress' curtain on a beaded pole

roman blinds...

- a 'dress' curtain with plenty of crystals

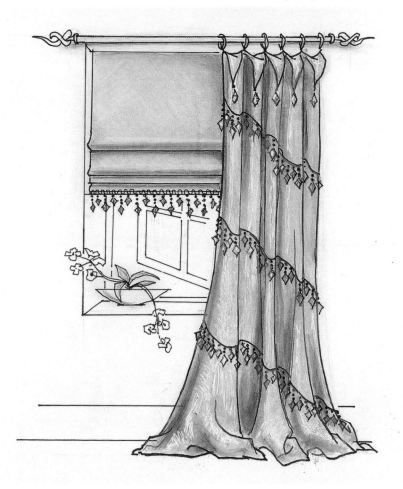

roman blinds...

- let the fabric take over

roman blinds...

-difficult shapes will need a template

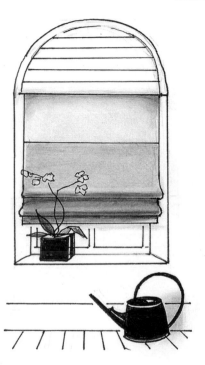

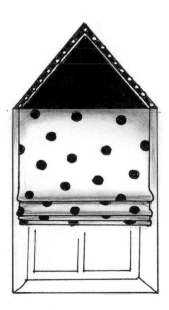

roman blinds...

- hand painted blossom

roman blinds...

- a picture window and translucent blinds

austrian blinds

As a general rule Austrian blinds
are handmade and they should be lined, unless you are
using a loose weave or a
translucent fabric. The blinds hang from a fabric covered
batten or pencil pinch pleated
heading tape is attached to the batten by a 'touch and
close' tape, they are pulled up by
cords which pass through china barrels and then secured
by a brass or chrome cleat. They
can also be operated electrically with a remote control.
I don't particularly like Austrian
blinds, as they are fussy and the fabric looks too
creased when in the down position,
but sometimes using the right fabric and in the right
room setting they can look amazing.
My advice is to keep them as simple as possible – the
plainer the better!

austrian blinds...

- with frilled hem

- with traditional wooden pelmet

austrian blinds...

- with carved wooden pelmet

austrian blinds...

austrian blinds...

austrian blinds...

- with pleated heading

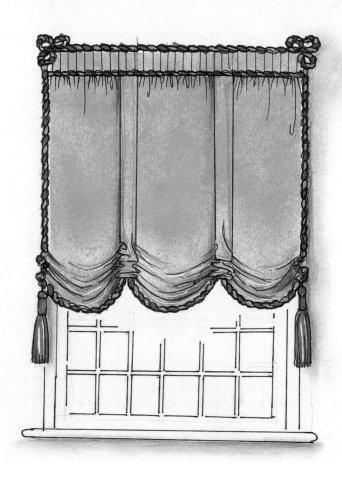

austrian blinds...

- with beaded pelmet

austrian blinds...

- fretwork pelmet and translucent blind

austrian blinds...

austrian blinds...

- edged with lace

austrian blinds...

- charming in a child's nursery

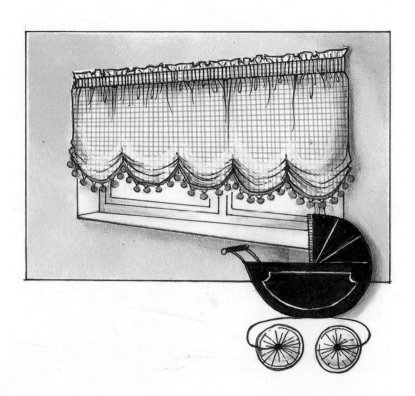

austrian blinds...

- black lace — looks spectacular!

austrian blinds...

austrian blinds...

- with quilted pelmet

austrian blinds...

If like me you don't particularly like
Austrian blinds but your client insists on them - then
comprimise... keep the Austrians
very simple and use together with panels or dress
curtains and the windows can look
quite amazing ... on the next few pages you will see
some examples.

austrian blinds...

- keep the blind very plain and add an interesting 'dress' curtain

austrian blinds...

- tartan blind and 'dress' curtain edged with Bullion fringe

austrian blinds...

austrian blinds...

linen fold

These blinds are completely
unstructured and I like the way they add a
natural look to a contemporary
room setting.
There are no rods or poles and
unlike Romans they are not 'trained' and
therefore fall in a relaxed style. As
the centre fabric is often voile or an open
weave avoid having any seams
across the fabric so maximum achievable
width will be the width of your
fabric generally about 180 cm(72") wide but
there is no restriction on length.
The borders are in a solid fabric, such as
linen, and the eyelet holes down
the side have the cord threaded in and out
which when pulled makes the blind
go into folds.

linen fold...

– open weave fabric with linen borders

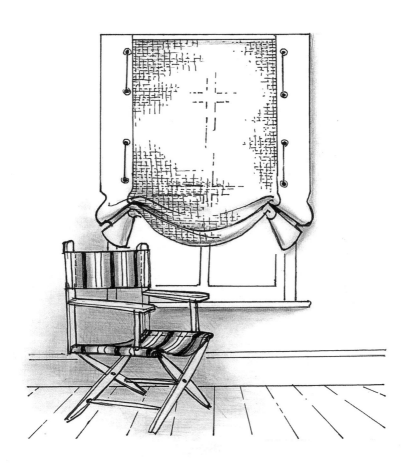

- with a valance and bobble trim

linen fold...

-in a garden room

linen fold...

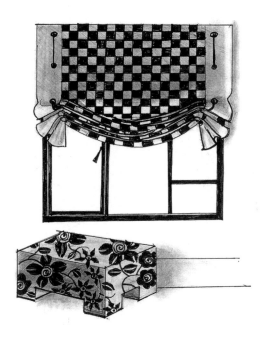

linen fold...

- a long thin window with a translucent fabric to 'dress it up'

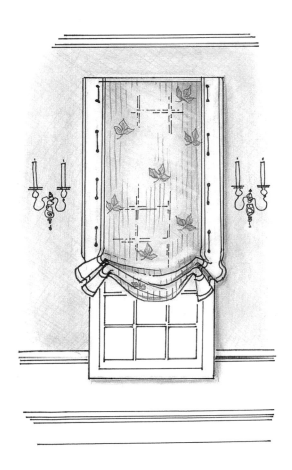

linen fold...

- gingham voile for the kitchen

linen fold...

-an open weave blind to let in the light

linen fold...

- with a fretwork pelmet

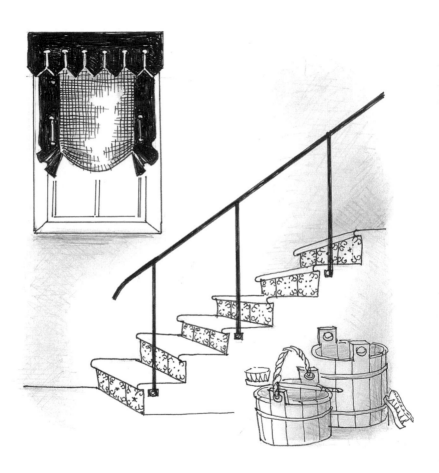

linen fold...

- works well in place of 'net curtains'

cascades....

Cascades are a more formal
version of a Roman blind, but unlike a Roman blind
they retain their folds when the
blind is down.
A cascade is handmade and
attached to a covered batten by a 'touch and close'
tape separated by lift cords which
pass through china barrels and secured by a brass
cleat. The pleats retain their
shape and precision by steel rods which are
inserted into horizontal pockets.
Additional cording retains the regular folds when
the blind is in the down position.
Avoid using cascades in bay windows as they are
too bulky. If you are using an
unlined translucent fabric the system may show
through — it might be best to use
a simpler Roman blind in this case.

cascades...

- quite a formal blind with neat folds

cascades...

- mixture of small prints with matching paper border

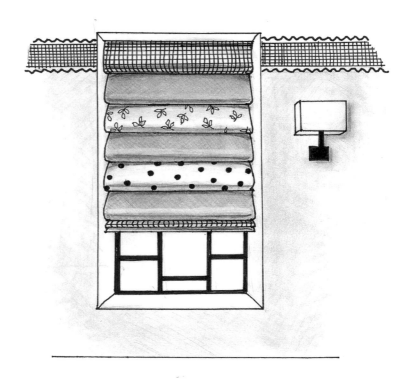

cascades...

- simple two toned blind

cascades...

– blends in well in a formal setting

cascades...

– a formal valance edged with a heavy bullion fringe

cascades...

- lambrequin with Russian braid trim

cascades...

- lambequin with a diagonal print

cascades...

- contrast borders

cascades...

- a double window with one pelmet

THE BLINDS CAN BE HIDDEN BEHIND THE
PELMET DURING THE DAY

x

cascades...

- a double window with one pelmet

THE BLINDS CAN BE HIDDEN BEHIND THE
PELMET DURING THE DAY

cascades...

- the neat folds of the blind look good with panels

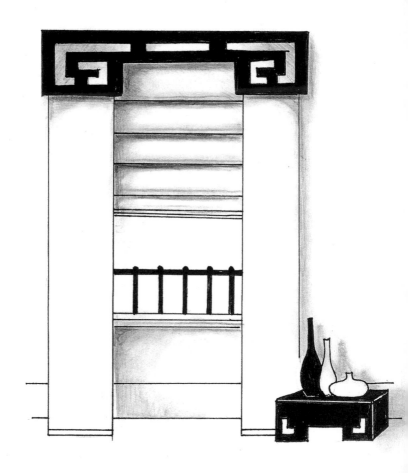

cascades...

- uncluttered lines to show off the print

cascades...

- patterned shawl thrown over a pole

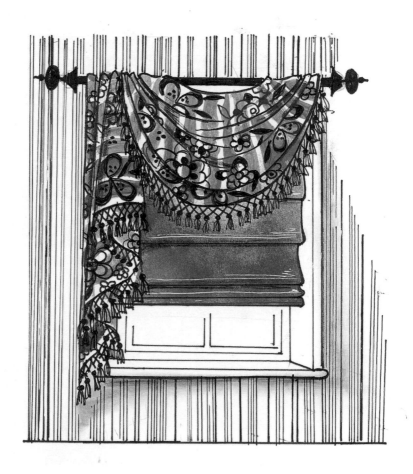

cascades...

- wrought iron pelmet with matching 'balcony'

cascades...

- use a strong unlined coloured lace with matching beads

cascades...

- add a few trimmings

cascades...

cascades...

- a soft valance with fringing or a beaded braid

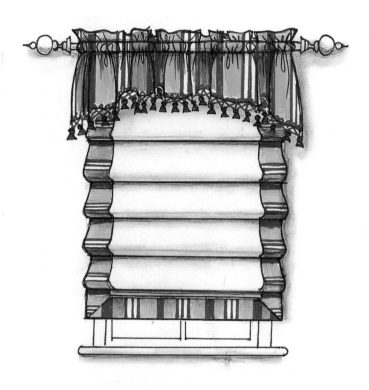

oriental blinds....

Oriental blinds are the simplest of all
the blinds, they are rolled up and drawn by cords which pass
through rings, the cords can be in a
contrast or matched to the top fabric colour. If they are
to be unlined remember to have
'French Seams' as the back of the blind will be seen from
the outside.

Normally an Oriental blind is 'bagged
out' – there are two fabrics, one for the top and a
contrast for the back, so fabric
quantities are equal. It is a good idea to add a machine hem
stitch to the edge of the two fabics if
the fabrics are thick and press well so that they roll up and
down easier.

oriental blinds...

-using a bold chevron print

143

oriental blinds...

-using a bold chevron print

oriental blinds...

- rely on the fabric

oriental blinds...

- together with Japanese style panels

oriental blinds...

- a 'dress' curtain and fretwork pelmet

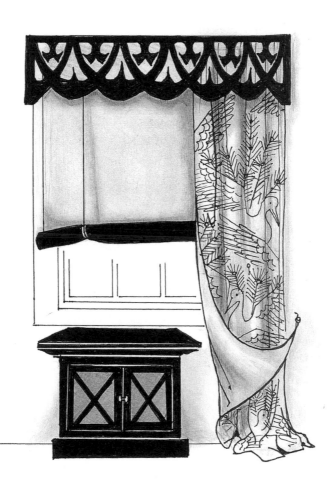

oriental blinds...

- try 'pinking' the edges of the blind – looks good and saves time!

oriental blinds...

- for a boys' room

oriental blinds...

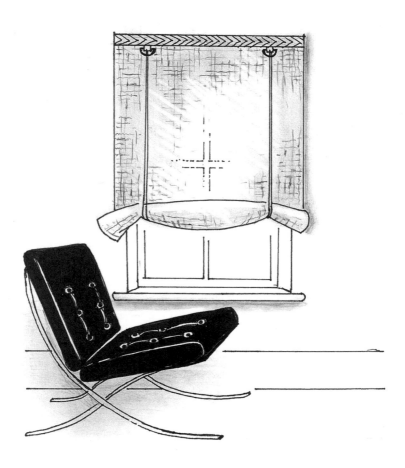

oriental blinds...

- for a long thin window

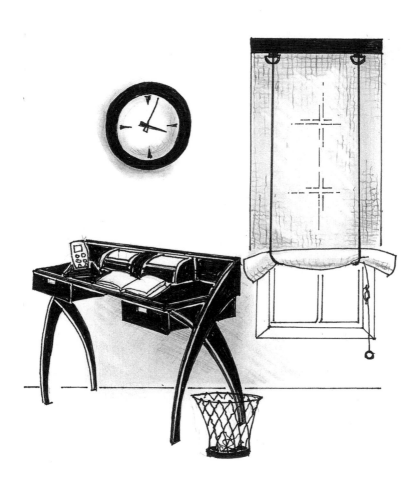

london blinds...

This is quite a formal 'period'
blind and it looks the part when it is lined, interlined
and with contrast inverted pleats.
Used mainly to 'dress' a window -perhaps in a hall
or on a landing, alone or teamed
up with other window treatments, but it does need
to be positioned properly or it
can look very messy! London blinds can be useful to
'dress' bay windows and also
solves the problem of arched windows – but you
need to give your manufacturer a
template of the shape.

london blinds...

- you will need to make a template for the shape at the top

london blinds...

- looks good in a traditional style room

london blinds...

- with a valance

london blinds...

- inverted pleats and plenty of trimming

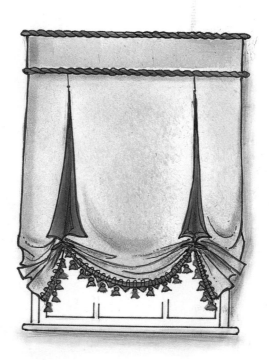

- contrast inverted pleats

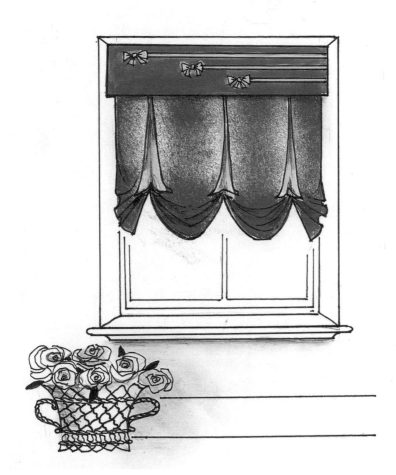

london blinds...

- for an awkward shape you need to make a template

london blinds...

- an arched window always causes problems

london blinds...

- with a bold patterned pelmet

- contrast edged valance and blind

I don't really believe there is still a place for
this blind except in a theatre maybe!

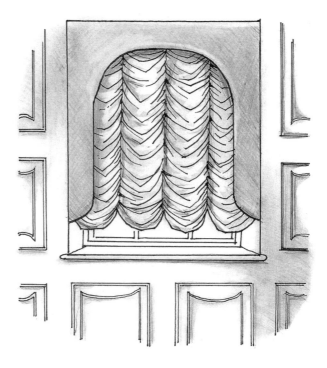

festoon blind...

- they look better when the strings have broken, a sort of faded glory!

Velux windows...

- as the family grows up, and you find that you need more room, try opening up the space in the roof and by putting in Velux windows you can create a completely new area for bedrooms and bathrooms – or maybe an office.

Velux blinds...

- convert the attic into an office

Velux blinds...

- make a bathroom in the attic and add a Velux window

conservatories...

SOME ADVICE — MANY MANUFACTURERS MAKE BLINDS ESPECIALLY
FOR CONSERVATORIES EITHER LIKE THESE SHUTTERS OR IN
VARIOUS TYPES OF FABRICS — HAND THE MEASURING OVER TO
THEM, STAND BACK AND LET THEM TAKE OVER!

shutters...

- these indoor 'Colonial' style shutters
are one of the most versatile types of window covering on
the market.   They are permanently
fixed to the windows and can be hinged back completely
or left in situ and the louvers moved
to an open or closed position manually. By moving the
louvers you can fine tune the amount
of light coming into the room and when in the closed
position, for privacy, they also give a
sense of security. Shutters can be spray painted any
colour to tie in with the décor or
supplied in various kinds of wood such as Mahogany,
Cherry, Oak, Beech or Pine and the
louvers come in 3 sizes 4.8 cms ($1\frac{7}{8}$") 6.4 cms ($2\frac{1}{2}$") and
8.9 cms ($3\frac{1}{2}$")
- but sizes vary from one manufacturer to another.
Frames come in different thicknesses
depending on the size of the shutters and you can
have a middle rail which should be
aligned with any window features. Shutters not only work
well in bay windows , as sketched on
the opposite page, but also can be custom made to fit any
awkward shaped windows – use them
in conservatories, in Velux windows and as wardrobe
doors – there is a place somewhere
for them in every house!   I buy my clients shutters from
a particular manufacturer in London
who plants two trees for everyone cut down to make
their shutters – a nice thought!

shutters...

- two tiered shutters work well in bay windows

shutters...

- much neater than curtains

shutters...

- can be made to fit any shape of window

shutters...

- a clean neat solution for an awkward shaped window

shutters...

- wider slats are my favourite

shutters...

shutters...

-'café' style wooden shutters

shutters...

-be adventurous when choosing your colours!

shutters...

– can be used in place of a Velux blind

wooden Venetian blinds...

- there is nothing new about wooden
slatted blinds but they have gained in popularity recently as
they do lend themselves to the more
contemporary décor that is so sort after at the moment.
Suitable for most windows they are
used just as much in offices as in homes, not just
because they look right, but because
they allow you to control the amount of light you let into
a room, stopping glare on the screen
of a computer as well as saving your soft furnishings
from fading if in direct sunlight. I prefer
the natural wooden blinds with jute webbing, but there
are limitless combinations…..any colour
you desire, marbled effect, mock suede and one
manufacturer even makes them in
leather! The width of the slats varies depending on the
size of the window and your
preferences - and you can have striped, checked or
flowered braids so that they tie in with
your colour scheme.
Wooden blinds should not be wider
than 1.8m (6') –anything wider than this you would
be advised to have 2 blinds.
Care and maintenance….dust with an ostrich feather
duster or use the brush attachment on
you vacuum cleaner. You can also buy a spray can of
compressed air from supermarkets
and hardware stores.

venetian blinds...

- wooden blinds in a natural colour with jute webbing is the winner!

Venetian blinds...

- can be used for glass doors as well as windows

venetian blinds...

- the slats can be made any colour and in various widths

Venetian blinds...

- popular in the 60's and 70's the Venetian blind is back in fashion!

They look particularly wholesome when in a natural wood with jute webbing. Although these blinds are 'dust collectors' and are not the easiest blinds to clean, they are widely used in homes and also in offices – they can be used for the back of glass doors which is very useful.

venetian blinds...

- they look good in black

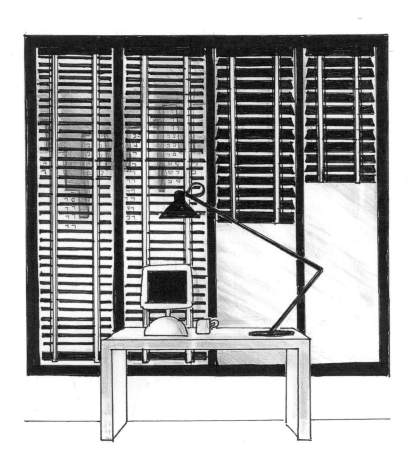

metal venetian blinds...

- the slats can be shaded as the sketch below

- these blinds come in a multitude of colours but these shaded ones are fun – they also look fabulous in silver. The slats come in 3 sizes 5cms (2") 2.5cms (1") and best of all 1.25cms (½") - some manufacturers make perforated slats which look very futuristic.

metal venetian blinds...

- a neat solution for tiny windows

panels...

these can hang as a wall decoration
from a pole, used as a room divider or better still hung
from the ceiling on aluminium tracking
as a replacement for curtains or blinds. Sliding panels are
derived from Japanese paper screens
and are designed to stack behind each other to give a
simple layering effect, The amount of
ceiling tracks depends on the amount of panels required
– a single track for one panel, two
for a double panel and so on. The fabric is attached at
the top with 'touch and close' tape
and if the fabric is lightweight I suggest you ask for
weights to be added at the hem.
Panels should not be wider than 90 cms (36 inches) and
can be electronically operated.

panels...

- three panels stacked to one side during the day

panels...

- show off a flamboyant brocade

panels...

- totally simple window covering even for a difficult window!

panels...

- a simple solution for french doors

panels...

- a large picture window with geometric prints

panels...

- the panels can slide away to the sides so the view is totally visable

panels...

- many homes are now in converted churches

panels...

- just simple but to the point

panels...

- perfect for a loft apartment

panels...

– continue the wallpaper and border on to this hardboard panel

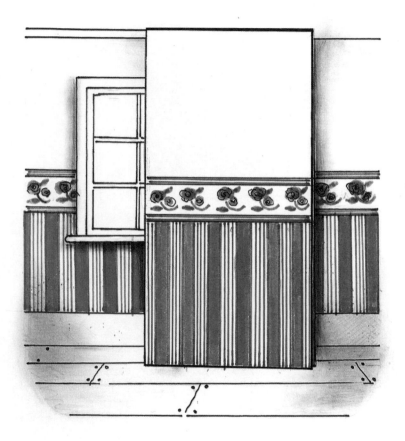

panels...

- can be used as a pin board too!

panels...

- 3 tones of plain fabric

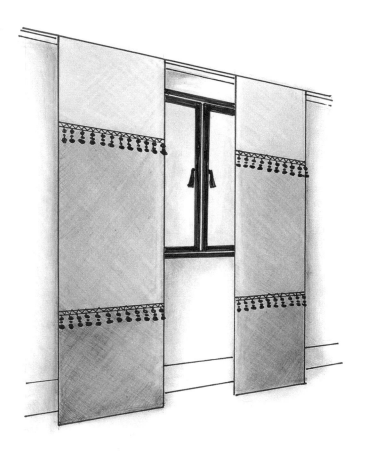

panels...

- trim the panels with a mixture of wide ribbons

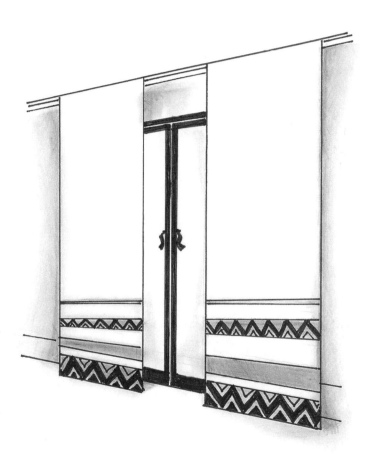

panels...

- with insets of lace

panels...

- eyelet holes and laces

panels...

- scalloped headings work well

panels...

- scalloped heading with the inset of Paisley print

panels...

- a single lace panel looks wonderful!

panels...

- a single panel in an open weave fabric

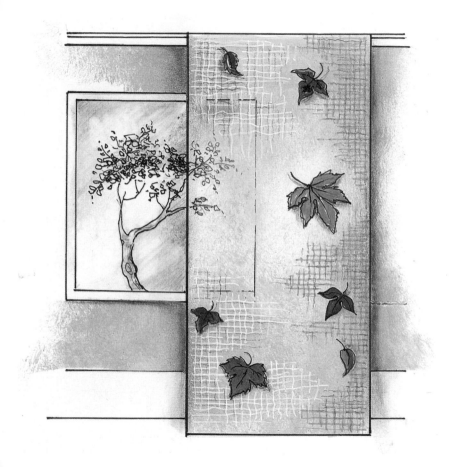

panels...

- two long panels + two centre panels

panels...

panels...

- use them for cupboards to hide the mess

panels...

- look good when used for wardrobe doors

portiéres...

- this kind of window covering is
generally used when the window opens into the
room making it difficult to have a
blind or curtains..special rods are
attached to the back of a window frame, or
door, and the fabric, with pocket
headings at the top and bottom, is then slotted
on to the rods - these rods are
on hinges so that they open and
close on the actual window frame.

portiéres...

- initialled linen with hem stitching

portiéres...

- plain and simple

portiéres...

- muslin slotted onto portiére rods

portiéres...

- can be embroidered with any pattern you wish

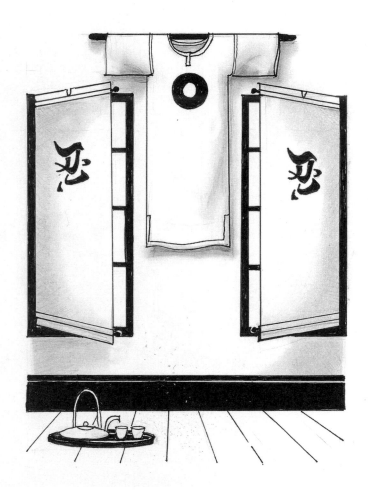

portiéres...

- spotted voile gathered onto rods

portiéres...

- can fold back against the wall on either side

portiéres...

- a single portiére attached to the frame of this French window

dormer windows...

– these windows are put into a roof
of an house in order to allow light into the loft so that
the wasted space can be used as an
additional room – this only works if the roof has a high
pitched roof so that you can stand up!

- an open weave roman blind with wide mitred bands

dormer windows...

- an old beamed loft with a simple linen fold blind

dormer windows...

dormer windows...

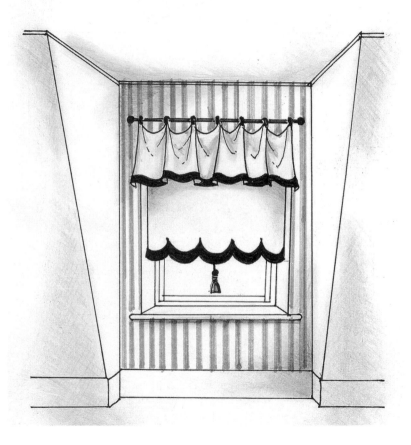

dormer windows...

difficult windows...

– sometimes, when faced with certain
difficult shaped windows, and there are many of them, I
make the decision to leave the
window completely bare as it can look ridiculous putting
an obviously contrived type of blind
or curtain – and it actually draws attention to the
problem – here are a few ideas that I
have used in the past to get me out of
trouble!

- a long thin window with a lambrequin and a lace blind to defuse the light

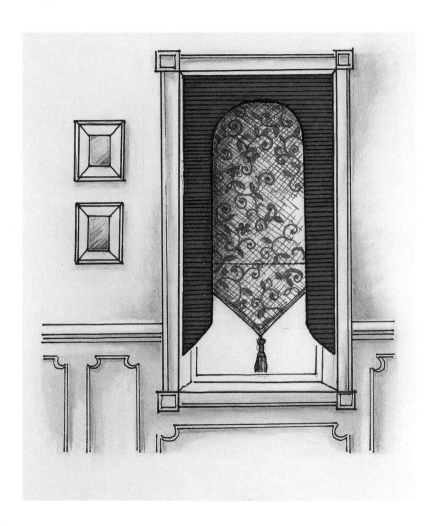

- a few examples of plissé blinds

– THESE BLINDS CAN BE MADE TO FIT EVEN THE MOST AWKARD SHAPES.

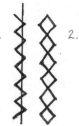

1.   2.

SIDE VIEW
OF BLINDS

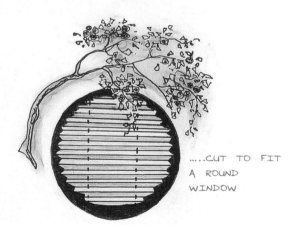

.....CUT TO FIT
A ROUND
WINDOW

1. A SINGLE PLISSÉ BLIND
2. HONEYCOMB BLIND –   EXTRA INSALLATION AND
   LIGHT RESISTANT

....THESE BLINDS ARE ALSO AVAILABLE IN DOUBLE FABRIC SO THAT, EVEN IF YOU HAVE A DIFFERENT COLOURED BLIND IN EACH ROOM, THE BACKING CAN BE A NEUTRAL SHADE TO LOOK UNIFORM ON THE OUTSIDE.

difficult windows...

- a plissé blind pulled up to make a café curtain

— BLINDS CAN BE CUT TO ANY SHAPE TO FIT THE MOST UNUSUAL SHAPED WINDOWS

-an enormous window

— WHEN A WINDOW IS THIS LARGE IT CAN BE VERY COSTLY TO HAVE CURTAINS OR A BLIND — A SCREEN LIKE THIS CAN SAVE THE DAY!

difficult shapes...

- cover the whole wall with just one enormous translucent blind

- UNLESS THE FABRIC IS EXTREMELY WIDE yOU WILL NEED TO HAVE FRENCH SEAMS - TRY TO HAVE THE SEAMS IN LINE WITH THE LINES OF THE WINDOW, AS yOU CAN SEE IN THE SKETCH ABOVE

difficult shapes...

- leave these windows alone

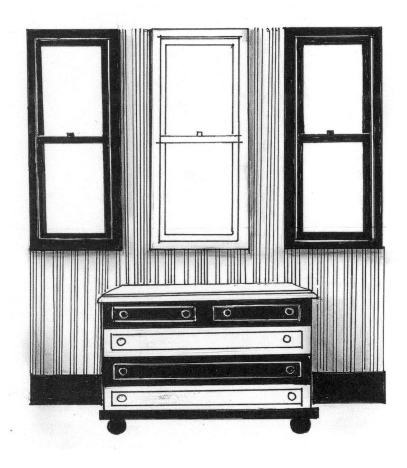

- JUST PAINT THE FRAMES TO MATCH YOUR FURNITURE

difficult shapes...

- narrow windows like these look best with plain white shutters

difficult shapes...

- JUST TREAT THEM AS ONE WINDOW AND THE PROBLEM IS SOLVED

difficult shapes...

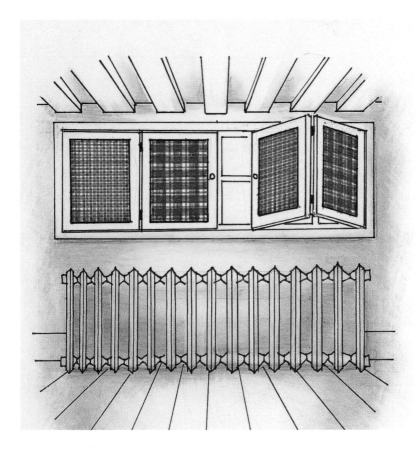

~ YOU CAN HAVE FABRICS FRAMED AND MADE INTO
HINGED SCREENS WHICH FOLD RIGHT BACK WHEN OPEN

dressing a window...

- it's not necessary to cover every
window automatically – some windows are better left
alone – perhaps the view is
spectacular or the architrave is period and elegant in
which case just 'dress' the window

dressing a window...

- a beaded curtain always looks stunning

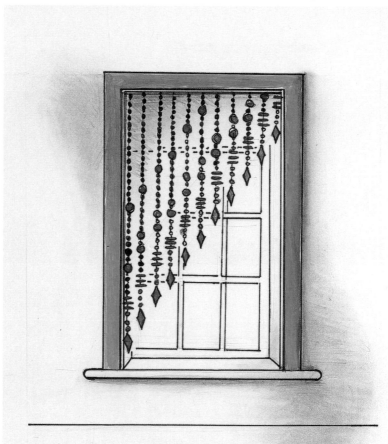

dressing a window...

- this idea was taken from the Savoy theatre in London

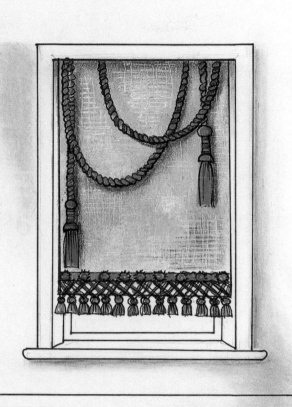

dressing a window...

- a pretty valance on a steel pole with plenty of trimmings

dressing a window...

-continue the wall border across the window
(if it's a non functional window)

dressing a window...

- a simple stencilled flower to match the other furnishings

dressing a window...

- fix an antique piece of lace to the window frame

dressing a window...

- emphasize the shape of this Georgian window with painted lines

alternative
window coverings...

- if you need to cover your windows and for some reason or another you don't want to use a conventional curtain or blind – try experimenting – use stencilling for instance or fix a wonderful print up at the window there are so many alternative ideas to choose from.

alternative window coverings...

alternative window coverings...

BAIN

alternative window coverings...

.....- these shutters fold back against the wall when open

alternative window coverings...

alternative window coverings...

- heavily fringed shawl simply tied up at the window

- a screen with a mixture of fabrics can have many different uses!

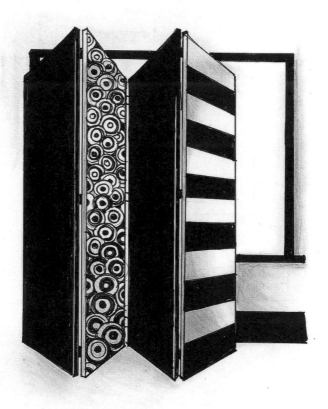

alternative window coverings...

TO HANG OVER A PICTURE WINDOW AT NIGHT!

fabric details...

On the following pages I have listed
the fabric and trimming suppliers names and reference
numbers – then from page 276 the
suppliers contact details. Contact them direct and they
will give you the name and address of
your nearest stockist.

fabric details...

- the basics

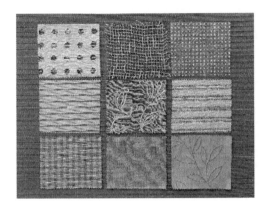

1. John England JE648D Linen and Polyester
2. John England JE412   Linen and Cotton
3. Blind Fashion - Quad Icicle – 100% Polyester
4. Blind Fashion Stripey - string 1282
5. Shelia Coombes - Rajput 03 – Linen and Chenille
6. Malabar – NSIL/10 – Silk
7. Malabar – Natural Chamba check – Cotton
8. Blind Fashion – Irish Linen 001 – Linen
9 Jane Churchill J359F-05 – Silk

fabric details...

- naturals

1. Schumacher/Greeff – Abigail Crewel GRF3296031-
   100% Cotton
2. Schumacher/ Greeff – Newport poplin 1230071
3. Schumacher/Greeff   - Wentworth Crewel GRF3300032 -
   100% Cotton
4. Brian Yates – Silkson 1110003-02 – Silk
5. Samuel & Son – 977 33280-91 - Jute
6. Samuel & Son – 987-12725-05 - Jute

fabric details...

- browns

1. Schumacher – 50700   Woodward Satin Stripe – Cotton & Silk
2. Schumacher – 50940 Houndstooth – Cotton & Cotton Chenille
3. Osborne & Little – F5272/03 - Viscose & Polyester
4. Wemyss Houles – Opaline 33264/9520
5. Wendy Cushing – Tassel 32612/06

fabric details...

- damson

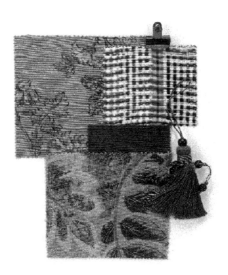

1. Anna French – Mandarin with parasol 82 - linen/cotton/nylon
2. Brian Yates – Hothouse Bermuda GT-04 - Cotton Polyester
3. Anna French – Palm Tree 63 - Linen & Cotton
4. Anna French – Vera Wheat 93 – Cotton & Linen
5. Wemyss Houles - beaded key tassel - Opaline 35211

fabric details...

- burgundy

1. Brian Yates – Poppyfield 137/02 - Linen & Viscose
2. Brian Yates – Herbert B8/01 - Linen & Viscose
3. Brian Yates – William B2/02 - Linen & Viscose
4. Brian Yates – Samuel B3/01 - Linen & Viscose
5. Nina Campbell – Follies Fringe NTC 473/01

fabric details...

1. Jane Churchill – Fairford J372F-01 – Viscose/linen
2. Malabar – Monga Tickle 18 - Silk
3. Zimmer & Rohde – Ginza 1809248635 – Silk
4. Jane Churchill Fairford J372F01 – Viscose/linen
5. Jane Churchill Audley stripe J37F/03 – Viscose/linen
6. Nye Nordiska – Ricombo /35 - Linen Voile

fabric details...

- scarlet

1. Nordic Style – Check – Linen & Cotton
2. Nordic Style – Plain – Linen & Cotton
3. Nordic Style – Dog Rose – 100% Linen
4. Nordic Style – Stripe – Linen & Cotton
5. Nordic Style – Big Check – Linen & Cotton
6. Wendy Cushing – Tassel custom made

fabric details...

1. Cath Kidston – Daisy – Cotton Duck
2. Cath Kidston – Stripe – Cotton Duck
3. Cath Kidston – Block Print – Cotton
4. Cath Kidston – Spot – Cotton Duck

fabric details...

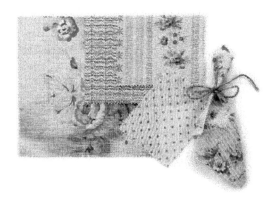

1. Brian Yates – Rambling Rose EL/01 100% Cotton
2. Brian Yates – Spring E7/01 – 100% Cotton
3. Cabbages & Roses – Blue Spot – Cotton
4. Brian Yates – Rosehip Stripe E6/01 – 100% Cotton
5. Brian Yates – Kashmir Rose ES/01 – 100% Cotton

fabric details...

- lilacs

1. Cath Kidston – FC12253 – Linen Union
2. Cath Kidston – FC41997 – Linen Union
3. Cath Kidston – FC42161 – Cotton
4. Malabar – Kenka Birch – Silk
5. Malabar – Kenka Rattle – Silk
6. Wemyss Houles – beaded key tassel – Opaline 35211

fabric details...

- pinks

1. Cabbages & Roses – Bees – Linen
2. Malabar – Kenka Birch – 100% Silk
3. Cabbages & Roses – Gingham – 100% Cotton

fabric details...

1. Nina Campbell – NCF3633/01 – 100% Cotton
2. Nina Campbell – NCF3631/01
3. Nina Campbell – NCF3630/01
4. Nina Campbell – NCF3632/01
5. Wemyss Houles - beaded key tassel – Opaline 35211
6. Nina Campbell – NCT432/01

fabric details...

- silks

1. Colefax & Fowler – F2301/06 – Silk
2. Jane Churchill – J359F/01
3. Zimmer & Rohde – Ginza 1809248635 – Silk
4. Nina Campbell – NCF3621/01 – Rayon & Silk Voile
5. Zimmer & Rohde – 1860251668 – 100% Silk
6. Nina Campbell – NCT473/04
7. Nina Campbell – NCT433/01 – Rope

fabric details...

- shocking pink & lime

1. Zimmer & Rohde – Etamine 18, 9245.735 - 100% Cotton
2. Zimmer & Rohde – 18,6025.775 – Silk
3. Nya Nordiska – Thuba/13 – Silk
4. Zimmer & Rohde – 1809247.735 – Silk
5. Zimmer & Rohde – Pinceau 1089250-392 - Linen Voile

fabric details...

- black with grey

1. Designers Guild – F1171/08 – Viscose and Linen
2. Wemyss Houles – Romance 05 – Acrylic/Viscose/Linen
3. Designers Guild – F1170/02 – Viscose & Linen
4. Wemyss Houles – luxury key tassel 35255/9900 -

-details

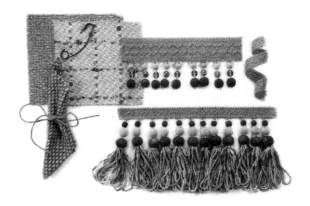

1. Malabar –Hopsack – 100% Jute
2. Brian Yates – Silksin 1110003/02 – Silk
3. Malabar – Indian Silk – Silk
4. Samuel & Son – Wide Jute Braid – 977-33280/91
5. Samuel & Son – Narrow Jute Braid – 977-33277/91
6. Samuel & Son – Beaded Fringe – 979-32672/S5
7. Samuel & Son – Beaded Tassel Fringe – 979-32671/S5

trimmings...

-details

1. Schumacher Houndstooth – 50944 –
   Cotton & Cotton Chenille
2. Wendy Cushing Trimmings – Crewel Braid 39809/04
3. Wendy Cushing Trimmings – Floral Range 39095/02
4. Wendy Cushing Trimmings – Floral Range 39094/02

trimmings...

-details

1. Brian Yates – William B2-01 Linen/viscose
2. Wemyss Houles – Wide braid – Polama 3242/9416
3. Wemyss Houles – Key Tassel – Polama 9416
4. Wemyss Houles – Cut Fringe – Polama 33267/9416
5. Wemyss Houles – Cut Fringe with hangers –
   Polama 33125/9416

trimmings...

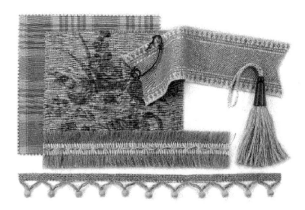

1. Colefax and Fowler - F2304/02 – Silk
2. Jane Churchill – Rosehurst – J382F/01 Viscose & Linen
3. Osborne & Little – Wide Braid – T544/01
4. Osborne & Little – Double edged fringe – T540/01
5. Samuel & Son – Wooden Bead Trim – 974 31738

glossary...

- the meaning of things

ARCHITRAVE.... the moulding around a door or window

AUSTRIAN BLINDS....a blind which is pulled up by cords which pass through china barrels – the fabric 'crunches up' when open (see page 94)

BASTE..... a running stitch – tacking

BATTEN.... wooden support for blinds

BAY WINDOW....an angled window which projects out of the room.

BRACKET.... wooden or metal support for poles or blinds

BRAID.....a narrow or wide woven ribbon used for trimming.

BUCKRAM ....a coarse fabric used for stiffening the tops of curtains or blinds

BULLION FRINGE.....a thick fringing used for trimming

CAFÉ STYLE... a window covering that covers the bottom half of the window - for privacy

CASCADE BLINDS....a more formal version of a roman blind with fixed folds of fabric when in the down position (see page 124)

CLEAT.... a hook on which to tie the cord used for working blinds

DRAPES (U.S).... curtains (U.K.)

DRESS CURTAINS.... curtains that are purely for show and not functional

EYLET HOLE... a metal hole punched into fabric with an eyelet machine

FACING.... a strip of fabric used to cover raw edges

FAN EDGING.... a trimming with one side looped to form a scalloped edging like a fan

FESTOONS....a blind that is pulled up by strings to form a series of vertical swags

FRENCH SEAM....a double seam which encloses a raw seam

FRENCH DOORS...a pair of glazed doors leading on to the garden or patio

glossary...

FRETWORK....pierced pattern on a solid piece of wood used to make galleries on chinoiserie furniture or used as a pelmet at the top of a window frame

FINIAL.... decorative ends which are fitted to either end of a metal or wooden curtain pole at end contain the rings

HEADING ...the finish at the top of the blind where the heading tape is sewn on.

HEADING TAPE... tape which is used to gather the material at the top of curtains and blinds – the gathering varies depending on the kind of tape used.

HEM... the turn up at the bottom of a pair of curtains or a blind

HERRINGBONE STITCH ...... used to neaten the edge of fabric

ITALIAN STRINGING.... a method of pulling back and up a curtain by means of stringing in a particular way

INTERLINING.....a soft wadding type of fabric which is put between the face fabric and the lining to add and extra thickness to the curtains or blind.

LAMBREQUINS.... A covered pelmet that also extends down the side of the window frame - .(see page 40)

LAMINATED....fabrics which are coated to give them more body

LEADING EDGE.... the centre edges of a pair of curtains

LINEN FOLD.... an unstructured blind mostly made with a translucent fabric in the centre (see page 114)

LINING..... a secondary fabric used to back the face fabric

LONDON BLIND.... A formal blind which is pulled up by cords passing through china barrels – more of a 'dress' blind than a functional one (see page 152)

MITRE..... the diagonal join of two pieces of fabric formed at a corner

ORIENTAL BLINDS....simple 'roll up' blinds – rolled up and down by cords which pass through rings (see page 142)

glossary...

PANELS....pieces of fabric with no fullness in them which hang from the ceiling by tracking – used as a replacement for curtains or blinds. derived from Japanese paper screens - they slide across the window and when in an open position can be stacked behind each other (see page 186)

PASSEMENTERIE....the French word for trimmings

PELMET.... a fabric covered shaped piece of board attached to the wall with brackets to hide the tracking

PENCIL PLEAT.... a tape is sewn to the top of curtains, or a blind, and when the strings of the tape are pulled a neat gathering is formed

PINKING....cut with pinking sheers for a regulated jagged edge

PLISSÉ.... a concertina pleated blind (see page 226)

POCKET HEADING (U.K.) – Rod pocket (U.S.A.) ...two rows of stitching at the top of a pair of curtains or blind wide enough for a pole or rod to be passed through

POLE .... a wooden or metal rod from which a curtain hangs

PORTIÉRE ROD..... a specially made thin pole which swings through 180 degrees and is fixed to the back of a door or to the frame of a window with fabric slotted onto the rod.

RAW EDGE....the rough cut edge of a fabric

RECESS....where the blinds or curtains are fixed in the alcove of a window

ROLLER BLIND...fabric which is rolled up and down on a roller to cover a window. Fixed on metal pins at the top of a window (see page 50)

ROMAN BLIND....a fabric blind which is operated by a series of strings at the back and allows blind to fold neatly over a window (see page 70)

SELVEDGE....a narrow strip on the edge of fabric to prevent fraying

SHADES ...American word for blinds

SHEERS....(voiles or nets in U.K.) a fine translucent fabric made into curtains or blinds

glossary...

SHUTTERS....hinged wooden panels which are fitted to window frame (see page 168)

SLIP STITCH....used to stitch the folding edge of a fabric to another

SWING ARMS.... hinged metal rods fitted to a dormer window for curtains

STACK BACK....a place where curtains can rest without blocking the light i.e. either side of a window

STENCIL.... a cut out pattern which is placed on the wall or blind and filled in by dabbing paint effect to leave a silhouette

TAB....a narrow width of fabric which when turned over double forms a loop

TEMPLATE....a pattern cut from paper or card which is used to mark a specific outline on a piece of fabric

TRACKING.... a metal or plastic rail from which curtains or panels hung – can also be corded or electrically controlled

TRANCLUCENT.... a thin fabric that allows light into the room

TRIMMING....(pasementerie) – braids and decorative attachments for curtains and blinds

VALANCE.... a gathered or pleated 'skirt' which is hung from the front edge of a pelmet board or pole to conceal the tracking and heading

VELUX.... a trade name for a skylight window in a sloping roof

VELUX BLINDS ...blinds made to fit a Velux wi ndow – they look similar to a roller blind but are guided by cords fixed to the frame to stop the blind falling away from the sloping window

VENETIAN BLIND... a slatted blind made from wood, plastic or aluminium – the slats are pulled up by cords (see page 178).

VOILE (U.K.) sheers (U.S.A) translucent fabric

suppliers list...UK

FABRICS –

ANNA FRENCH
020 7351 1126
enquiries@annafrench.co.uk

ANDREW MARTIN
020 7225 5100
info@andrewmartin.co.uk

BERY DESIGNS
020 7924 2197
bery@dircon.co.uk

BRIAN YATES
020 7352 0123
sales@brian-yates.co.uk

BRUNSCHWIG & FILS
020 7351 5797
london@brunschwig.co.uk

CATH KIDSTON
020 7221 4248
info@cathkidston.co.uk

CABBAGES & ROSES
020 8878 3702
enquiries@cabbagesandroses.com

CHASE ERWIN
020 7352 7271
showroom@chase-erwin-freeserve-co.uk

COLEFAX & FOWLER
020 7351 0666
Chelsea.harbour@colefax.co.uk

DESIGNERS GUILD
020 7351 5775
info@designersguild.com

G.P. & J. BAKER
01202 266 700
sales@gpjbaker.co.uk

IKEA (RETAIL)
020 7722 0997

JANE CHURCHILL
020 7730 9847
Chelsea.harbour@colefax.co.uk

JOHN LEWIS (RETAIL)
020 7629 7711
Furnishingfabrics_oxford_street
@johnlewis.co.uk

KA INTERNATIONAL (RETAIL)
Interior stores world wide
0870 011 4334

KRAVET
020 7975 0110
kravetlondon@hotmail.com

LAURA ASHLEY (RETAIL)
0870 562 2116
Customer.services@lauraashley.com

MALABAR
020 7501 4200
info@malabar.co.uk

telephone for your nearest stockist...

NORDIC STYLE
020 7351 1755
sales@nordicstyle.com

NYA NORDISKA
020 7351 2783
Britain@nya.com

OSBORNE AND LITTLE
020 7352 1456
oandl@osborneandlittle.com

PONGEES
020 7739 9130
info@pongees.com

ROMO
01623 756699
sales@romofabrics.com

ROBERT ALLEN
01494 474741
sales@robertallendesign.co.uk

TURNELL & GIGON
(SCHUMACHER & GREEF)
020 8971 1711
sales@turnellgigon.com

ZIMMER & ROHDE
020 7351 7115
Info.uk@zimmer-rohde.com

ZOFFANY
08708 300 060
enquiries@zoffany.com

BLINDS (SHADES)

ALLISON WHITE
020 7609 6127
mail@allisonwhite.co.uk

AMERICAN SHUTTERS
020 8876 5905
info@americanshutters.co.uk

BLIND FASHION
01628 529676
sales@blindfashion.co.uk

COPES (wooden)
020 8884 5319
sales@copes.co.uk

HUNTER DOUGLAS
0161 442 9500
info@luxaflex-sunway.co.uk

HABITAT (RETAIL)
0870 411 5501
store.tcr@habitat.co.uk

HEALS (RETAIL)
020 7896 7451
customerservices@heals.co.uk

LUXAFLEX
0800 652 7799
info@luxaflex-sunway.co.uk

NEW HOUSE
01989 740684
info@newhousetextiles.co.uk

THE NEW ENGLAND SHUTTER
COMPANY
020 8675 1099
enquiries@tnesc.co.uk

THE BLINDS COMPANY
020 7627 0909
theblindscompany@compuserve.com

THE SHUTTER SHOP
01252 844575
sales@shuttershop.co.uk

THE HOUSE OF SHUTTERS
0845 230 1940
info@thehouseofshutters.com

SHUTTERCRAFT
0845 855 2004
sales@shuttercraft.co.uk

SILENTGLISS
01843 863571
info@silentgliss.co.uk

STYLELINE BLINDS
0800 068 7573
info@stylelineblinds.co.uk

SUNWAY
0161 442 9500
help@luxaflex-sunway.co.uk

TIDMARSH & SONS
01279 450556
sales@verticaltec.co.uk

TRIMMINGS (passementerie)

BRITISH TRIMMINGS
0161 480 6122
uk.sales@btrim.co.uk

CASTELLANO-BELTRAME
+ 39 031 334 7575
castbelit@castbel.co.za

COLEFAX AND FOWLER
020 7351 0666
chelsea.harbour@colfax.co.uk

JANE CHURCHILL
020 7730 9847
Chelsea.harbour@colfax.co.uk

OSBORNE AND LITTLE
020 7352 1456
oandl@osborneandlittle.com

PRICE AND COMPANY
01273 421 999
orders@price-regency.co.uk

SPINA
020 7328 5274
spinadesign@btinternet.com

V.V. ROULEAUX
sales@vvrouleaux.com

WENDY CUSHING
020 73515796
wcushing@btrim.co.uk

WEMMYS HOULES
020 736 4430
wemyss@
chelseaharbour.fsbusiness.co.uk

STENCILS

THE STENCIL HOUSE
01661 844844
sales@stencillibrary.com

LININGS/WORKROOM SUNDRIES

EDMUND BELL
01274 680000
sales@edmundbell.co.uk

JONES INTERIORS
0115 973 8710
info@jonesnottm.co.uk

JOHN LEWIS
RETAIL BRANCHES
THROUGHOUT U.K.
08456 049049

STREETS
01268 766677
sales@streets.co.uk

COMPONENTS FOR BLINDS

COPE AND TIMMINS
0845 45 88860
info@copeandtimmins.co.uk

PRETTY FRILLS
01869 897180
info@prettyfrills.co.uk

PRICE AND COMPANY
01273 421 999
orders@price-regency.co.uk

McCULLOCH AND WALLIS
(RETAIL)
020 7629 0311
mculloch@psilink.co.uk

RUFFLETTE
0161 998 1811
customercare@rufflette.com

STREETS
01268 7666 77
sales@streets.co.uk

POLES

COPE AND TRIMMINS
0845 45 88860
info@copeandtimmins.co.uk

FABRICANT
020 7263 7999
sales@fabricant.co.uk

suppliers list...UK

THE BRADLEY COLLECTION
0845 118 7224
info@bradleycollection.co.uk

HALLIS HUDSON
01772 202202
sales@hallishudson.com

HUNTER HIGHLAND
01372 378511
enquiries@hunterandhighland.co.uk

JONES INTERIORS
0115 973 8710
info@jonesnottm.co.uk

McKINNEY AND CO
020 7627 5077
sales@mckinney.co.uk

PRICE AND COMPANY
01273 421 999
orders@price-regency.co.uk

RUFFLETTE
0161 998 1811
customercare@rufflette.com

SILENTGLISS
01843 863 571
info@silentgliss.co.uk

SWISH
01827 64242
Graham.bremer@nr-europe.com

WALCOT HOUSE
01993 832940
walcot@dial.pipex.com

SHOWROOMS TO VISIT

CHELSEA HARBOUR
DESIGN CENTRE
020 7225 9149
enquiries@chelsea-harbour.co.uk

ASSOCIATIONS

BIDA (BRITISH INTERIOR
DESIGN ASSOCIATION)
020 7349 0800
enquiries@bida.ory

suppliers list...USA

FABRICS

ANDREW MARTIN
212 688 4498

ANNA FRENCH/HENRY CALVIN
617 737 0691

BEACON HILL
212 421 1200

BRUNSCHWIG & FILS
212 838 7878

COLEFAX AND FOWLER
212 753 4488

CATH KIDSTON
212 751 3333

COWAN AND TOUT
212 753 4488

DESIGNERS GUILD
212 751 3333

DONGHIA
1-800 – DONGHIA

G.P.J. BAKER
800 – 453 3563

HOLLY HUNT
212 755 6555

JANE CHURCHILL
212 753 4488

GREEFF
888. 298 2991

KRAVAT
800-648- KRAV

LEE JOFA
800 453 3563

NINA CAMPBELL
212 751 3333

NORDIC STYLE/ WHITEONWHITE
212 288 0909

NYA NORDISKA –
RANDOLF AND HEIN
212 826 9898

OSBORNE AND LITTLE
212 751 3333

SCHUMACHER
212 415 3900 / 800 332 3384

ROBERT ALLEN
212 421 1200

WAVERLY
800 423 5881

WESCO
212 355 5211 / 303 388 4101

ZIMMER AND ROHDE
212 627 8880

suppliers list...USA

ZOFFANY
800 395 8760

**POLES
(DRAPERY/HARDWARE)**

ABC CARPET AND HOME (RETAIL)
212 473 3000

FABRICANT
212 755 6700

CARLETON V LIMITED
212 355 4525

GRACIOUS HOME (RETAIL)
212 231 7800

HOME EXPO (RETAIL)
770 433 8211

JO-ANN (RETAIL)
330 463 6790 / 800 525 4951

KIRSCH
1-800 817 6344./ 800 538 6567

POTTERY BARN (RETAIL)
800 922 5507 / 800 922 5507

ROBERT ALLEN
8003020 / 212 421 1200

CALICO CORNERS (RETAIL)
610 444 9700

BLINDS (SHADES)

BECKENSTEIN HOME (RETAIL)
212 475 4887

blindsgalore.com
(large selection of blinds online)

colonialwindowtreatment.com.
(online blinds)
888 399 4947

Plantationshutters.com
212 752 1140

WINDOW MODES
212 752 1140

**LININGS - LIGHT RESISTANT/
FIRE RETARDENT**

HAYNES FABRICS COMPANY
800 430 8296

COMPONENTS FOR BLINDS

BECKENSTEIN HOME (RETAIL)
212 475 4887

GRACIOUS HOMES (RETAIL)
212 517 6300 / 212 231 7800

telephone for your nearest stockist...

TRIMMINGS (PASSEMENTERIE)

BRIMAR
800 274 1205

CONSO
864 427 9004

DONGHIA
1-800-DONGIA
HOULES
212 935 3923

JANE CHURCHILL
212 753 4488

SAMUEL AND SONS
212 704 8000

SCHUMACHER
212 485 3900

OSBORNE AND LITTLE
212 751 3333

SHOWROOMS TO VISIT

D&D BUILDING . . . NEW YORK

**PEACHTREE HILL AVENUE . . .
ATLANTA**

**PACIFIC DESIGN CENTER . . . WEST
HOLLYWOOD**

DESIGN CENTER . . . DALLAS

DESIGN CENTER . . . BOSTON

antique markets...

What to look for . . .

Tea towels (Les Tourchons) appeared first in the 13th century – crisp and simple, off white with red initials modestly cross-stitched in the corner. In the 19th century girls would embroider their own initials in the corner and when they were getting married they would add their finaces initials beside theirs!

Provencial fabrics (les Indiennes) electric coloured prints originally made in India, hand blocked and coloured with vegetable dye. They became very popular in the 60s and 70s copied by Souleido, who revived them but now perhaps a little passé.

Linens (le linge) white or off white – beautifully embroidered and edged with intricate laces. Very collectable – look for tea towels, pillow cases and table cloths – all can be adapted into window coverings PURE MAGIC

Where to Go . . .

If you live in France, as I do, you will find every little village has its own market day. Here are a few that I know:

Nice – every Monday big antique market - very good

Valbonne – 1st Sunday in every month - 3 very good linen stalls

St Tropez – every Saturday large market worth a visit

Antibes – Saturday mornings

Aix-en-Provence – Saturdays are best - worth a visit

L'Isle-sur-Sorge – Sundays - wonderful tiles too

Cannes – 1st Sunday of each month

Paris – Puces de St Ouen (porte de Clignancourt) wonderful flea market Saturday, Sunday and Monday.

antique markets...

UK MARKETS AND SHOPS

Alfie's Antique Market
020 7723 6066

Grays' Antique Market
020 7629 7034

Guinevere Antiques
020 7736 2917

Lunn Antiques
020 7736 4638 –
lunnantiques@aol.com

Dierdre's Shop – Talbot Walk – Ripley, Surrey

Tobias & the Angel – White Hart Lane, London, SW13

Portobello Market - Portobello Road, London W11 – Saturdays best

Kempton Race Course market - Sunbury, Surrey – 2nd & last Tuesday each month 01932 782 292

Sandown Racecourse market - Esher, Surrey – 0171 249 4050

The 3 below are sponsored by the Daily Mail. For details call 01636702 326

Ardingly - Sussex • Newark – Lincolnshire • Malvern – Worcestershire

notes...

notes...

acknowledgements...

...thank you Chrissie for your wonderful interpretations of my designs .....how have we managed to work together for so many years and be still speaking?...it must be in the stars!

A big thank you to all the people in the showrooms at Chelsea Harbour and to Emma at Malabar who cut the samples for me and to Stella at Wendy Cushing who sells so many of my books as well as being a friend.

To Marian and Wendy who are always there for me!

To Tony for perfect 'snaps' and Ray who has had to work hard to get this book on the road.

...and finally to Simon and everyone at CPD who pulled everything together for me!